THE INFJ HEART

Understand the Mind, Unlock the Heart

JENNIFER SOLDNER

The INFJ Heart:

Understand the Mind, Unlock the Herat

First Edition

© 2015 Jennifer Soldner

All rights reserved.

ISBN 978-1-517-27345-3

Dedicated to all those who have
reached out to me seeking
understanding and guidance
in their relationships.

Other books by

JENNIFER SOLDNER

The Empathic INFJ:
Awareness and Understanding for the Intuitive Clairsentient

The Empathic INFJ Workbook:
Tools and Strategies for the Intuitive Clairsentient

A Look Inside a Rare Mind:
An INFJ's Journal through Personal Discovery

Author's Note

When I was in college many years ago, I met the love of my life. Just as many young lovers, we worked our way through several rocky discussions, riddled with miscommunications and frustration. We stuck through our relationship, both focused on making it work. Looking back, I cannot help but wonder how much simpler our discussions would have flowed had we been aware of one another's Myers-Briggs personality types.

Much further along in our relationship, we discovered that he is an ISTJ and I am an INFJ. With this newfound knowledge, we were able to look back at past discussions, disagreements and miscommunications through the lens of understanding our cognitive processes. Moving forward, we recognized our differences and embraced our similarities, helping one another grow and strengthen, improving our ability to communicate and deepening our level of intimacy.

Since then, I have been committed to helping others understand their Myers-Briggs personality type, the cognitive functions it represents and how to apply this knowledge to their relationship. Through working one-on-one with many individuals, I began to see a pattern where most couples were struggling to understand their INFJ partners.

> ### Real Relationships
>
> Throughout the book, look for text boxes with words from real individuals in real INFJ relationships. Note that, to protect privacy, their identities have been concealed.

After seeing how the simple act of gaining knowledge of their partner's perspectives could transform relationships, I wanted to make this information available to anyone in the same position, whether struggling in their relationship or simply hoping to strengthen their level of intimacy and better understand the INFJ they love.

When we can learn how an individual communicates, comprehend how they see the world and step into their mind, empathy, patience and compassion grow and relationships can flourish. It is my hope that this book offers this level of insight about how the INFJ mind works, particularly in relation to their significant other, in order to strengthen communication. Only through understanding the INFJ mind are you able to unlock the secrets of their heart.

Jennifer Soldner

—CONTENTS—

Introduction

You have eyes for an INFJ. It is not surprising that you are seeking information to understand what makes them tick. Perhaps you recently met this person and are curious how to initiate a romance. Maybe you have known them for years and are still unsure of where you stand. Or perhaps you have been together, dating, married or in love for a while now and still find yourself perplexed on a regular basis.

You are certainly not alone. Odds are that the INFJ you are pining after has moments where they are just as confused about themselves.

INFJs are enigmas. Their wants and needs constantly seem to change. They hold the core of who they are within a deep and secretive garden; pieces gated and locked away sometimes even from themselves. Getting them to open up is a feat and finding a way to help them continue to open up is a treasure. They want to share every piece of themselves with you on the most intense and intimate level but they may find themselves frightened of doing so, and thus shut themselves up in an emotional tower, half wishing that you will slay the dragon of distrust and rescue them from their loneliness and half hoping you just move on.

However, if you are reading this book, odds are you have no intention of moving to the next tower. You have set your sights on this INFJ, for better or worse, and want to move forward, seeking a better understanding of who they are, how they think and what you can do to help them gain trust in you and offer you the beautiful level of intimacy you know they hold inside.

Every INFJ is different. Each one is a unique and magnificent human being with their own sets of strengths and weaknesses, wants and needs, and positive and negative traits. They all have a history within them that has developed their personality into who they are today.

There is no one formula to understanding or unlocking the heart of an INFJ, nor should you be looking for one. But with the right information paired with genuine interest and intentions, it is possible to forge ahead in your relationship, seeking understanding, open communication, mutual respect and above all, pure love for one another just as any relationship needs to survive.

It is important to understand that this book is merely a guide to help you learn the INFJ in your life, offering you a starting point in pursuing or strengthening the relationship and allowing you to better understand the complex and curious mind of an INFJ. It is not intended to be a magic, one-size-fits-all solution to the complicated realm of dating or marriage. How you use this information will make a big impact on the success of your relationship. No outside source, bank of information or general advice will or can ever replace the most important factor in any relationship: open and honest personal communication from both individuals involved.

As you read through this book, consider each piece as a launching point for current or future discussions. You may even consider reading it together if you are at a comfortable place in your relationship to do so. Learning about one another is a fabulous way for any couple to pursue or strengthen intimacy, so try not to make discovery a one-sided venture. Just as you are seeking deeper understanding of the INFJ in your life, so to should they be attempting to better understand you.

No matter which stage of the relationship you may currently be in, it is my hope that you can use the information in this book to help you better understand and communicate with the INFJ who catches your eye, helping you to comfortably and confidently unlock the secrets of the INFJ heart.

Myers' and Briggs' INFJ

In the 1940s, after extensively studying Carl Jung's theories of psychological types[1] based on his clinical analyses, two sisters, Katharine Cook Briggs and Isabel Briggs Myers, published the *Briggs Myers Type Indicator Handbook* which later became known as the "Myers-Briggs Type Indicator."[2]   The Myers-Briggs Type Indicator, also referred to as MBTI, has since been used as a tool to categorize and explain the different ways human brains receive and process information.

---

[1] Jung, Carl. *Psychological Types*. Princeton University Press, 1976.
[2] Briggs Myers, Isabel & Mary H. McCaulley. *Manual: A Guide to the Development and Use of the Myers-Briggs Type Indicator.* Consulting Psychologists Press, 1985.

INFJ is one of the sixteen types defined by Myers and Briggs. It stands for Introvert, iNtuitive, Feeling and Judicial. These terms are four of the eight dichotomies explained by Myers and Briggs.

Introvert ↔	Extrovert
iNtuitive ↔	Sensing
Feeling ↔	Thinking
Judging ↔	Perceiving

Using these dichotomies, Myers and Briggs were able to explain the personalities of individuals on a surprisingly accurate scale. They describe INFJs as individuals who:

"Seek meaning and connection in ideas, relationships, and material possessions. Want to understand what motivates people and are insightful about others. Conscientious and committed to their firm values. Develop a clear vision about how best to serve the common good. Organized and decisive in implementing their vision."[3]

---

[3] The Myers & Briggs Foundation. "The 16 MBTI Types." 2015. http://www.myersbriggs.org/my-mbti-personality-type/mbti-basics/the-16-mbti-types.htm.

Since the introduction of MBTI, many others have added their own descriptions, explanations and analyses to the fold, leaving us now with an even more in-depth picture of what it means to be an INFJ.

It is important to note, however, that while MBTI can be astonishingly descriptive on the whole, each person is an individual and thus no description will ever fit them entirely. MBTI is a great resource to discover how one's brain functions by explaining how they receive, process and deliver information. With this information, we are then able to make larger generalizations about how they may behave in certain circumstances. But when using this tool, it is important to never dismiss each individual's humanity, uniqueness and ability to exhibit different emotions, thoughts and behaviors than any book may define.

The INFJ Mind

The first step to any fulfilling relationship with an INFJ is to understand as much as you can about the personality type. Even though there is a lot to grasp about the INFJ type, it is helpful to start with a quick overview of what makes them tick. The best way to do this is to look at what are called cognitive functions.

The cognitive functions are the blueprint of each Myers-Briggs personality type. Every person has eight functions which are divided into four primary functions and four shadow functions. The order of the functions can tell you a lot about how a type's brain receives, processes and then delivers information.

Let us first look at the four primary functions of an INFJ. The first, or dominant, function of an INFJ is introverted iNtuition (Ni). The Ni function is the biggest part of what makes INFJs so unique. This function means that they have the ability to think more abstractly, globally, thoroughly and complexly. This allows the INFJ to easily see and understand things in the past, present and future that others may struggle to comprehend. Ni dominant personalities rely heavily on gut feelings and internal theories that appear to come out of nowhere. They pull information from an internal map which their mind has pieced together over time based on their personal experiences.

Being their dominant function, an INFJ's Ni process comes naturally to their line of thinking, often used consciously and thoroughly, and almost always in a positive way. The aspects of their lives that seem to come easily or in which they excel are usually rooted in their dominant function, though that may not be readily apparent as it works on an internal process, revealed only to those closest to them.

The secondary, or auxiliary, function of an INFJ is extroverted Feeling (Fe). The Fe function is what makes INFJs eager to please those around them. While their sense of self is wrapped up in their intuition, their sense of others runs mainly on a desire to connect with them through feelings. Extroverted Feelers tend to act in ways that make others feel comfortable and pleased, mainly through warmth, graces and good manners.

The auxiliary function is usually well-developed early on in life and works strongly in conjunction with the dominant function. These combined processes lead the INFJ to be people-oriented on a global level, causing them to take on quite a bit of personal responsibility for those around them.

The Fe function is what most initially see when meeting an INFJ as it runs on an external process. It can lead others to believe the INFJ is an extrovert, based on their outgoing nature and people-oriented focus.

The third function of an INFJ is introverted Thinking (Ti). This process is rooted in analyzing, internal reasoning and categorizing. While the dominant and auxiliary functions come naturally, the third function usually remains poorly developed until later on in life, exhibiting itself as a weak or negative point in one's thinking. Because of this, younger INFJs are likely to struggle with internal logic, leaving them more controlled by their Ni and Fe functions.

The fourth INFJ function is extroverted Sensing (Se) which refers to awareness of external sensory details and how one relates to the physical world around them. There is some debate on how personalities use their fourth function. One class believes, just as the third function, that the fourth remains poorly developed until one ages. Others believe that it is fully developed and accessed on a subconscious level from a ripe age, leaving it working in pristine fashion without conscious knowledge.

While we cannot be sure which theory is accurate, one thing that most agree on is that consciously, the fourth function appears to be weak and exhibits itself through the negative traits of our behavior. Because of this, the INFJ is less apt be actively aware of or interested in the physical world around them.

These four primary functions make up the majority of who the INFJ is on a day to day basis. With the knowledge of one's primary functions, it becomes easier to understand and, in some cases even predict their actions in any given situation.

The shadow functions are the weakest cognitive processes, usually working subconsciously. Due to the lack of development of the shadow functions, when they do become conscious, they tend to exhibit negative characteristics or dark sides of an individual's personality. To try to use these functions on a conscious level is mentally taxing, just like using a weak muscle.

The fifth through eight functions of an INFJ, in order, are:

- extroverted iNtuition (Ne) – interpreting hidden meanings, brainstorming ideas and interweaving small details to form a larger picture.

- introverted Feeling (Fi) – weighing information against a core belief system and assigning value and significance to all things.
- extroverted Thinking (Te) – organizing, sequencing and planning ideas and environments based on logic and facts.
- introverted Sensing (Si) – Storing and retrieving detailed facts and weighing them against current situations.

Knowing the full functional stack of any personality type can begin to tell you quite a bit about how they think and act. It is the first and most important step in understanding your partner. Later on in this book, I will offer a glimpse of the cognitive processes of each personality type so you will better be able to see how your stack compares with that of the INFJ.

The Human INFJ

Though the letters and functions of MBTI types can certainly appear cold and scientific, this phenomenal insight into the human mind can be translated into a beautifully accurate portrait of a human being. On the whole, INFJs are idealistic individuals with strong values which they prefer to apply to the greater good of humanity. Due to their dominant Ni function, the INFJ has an innate ability to process abstract information not readily available to most types. This helps them view the world in a unique way, comprising abstract scenarios and seeing fresh angles.

Combined with their auxiliary Fe function, the INFJ uses their intuitive abilities in humanitarian ways. They are naturally people-oriented and show very little interest in ideas which do not have a direct impact on improving humanity.

Though the INFJ has a deep longing to help others, as introverts, they also thrive in solitude, feeling overwhelmed and overexerted when they are unable to retreat for an appropriate amount of time. They often find themselves seeking the perfect balance between living to help others and living to hide from others.

Because of their poorly developed sensing functions, INFJs frequently struggle with normal day to day applications necessary in life from accounting and directions to housework and scheduling. It is not that they are necessarily bad at these things, but rather they can feel overwhelmed with the minutia of sensory details.

It is believed that INFJs make up the smallest percentage of the general population, approximately one to three percent.[4] Paired with their unique Ni dominant function, it is not uncommon for the INFJ to feel alone or different from those around them, even if they are unsure as to why.

A perfect combination of planning and chaos, people and solitude and dreaming and action, the INFJ regularly finds themselves to be a conflicting, or all

---

[4] Statistic was "compiled from a variety of MBTI® results from 1972 through 2002, including data banks at the Center for Applications of Psychological Type; CPP, Inc.; and Stanford Research Institute (SRI)." The Myers & Briggs Foundation. "How Frequent is My Type." 2015. http://www.myersbriggs.org/my-mbti-personality-type/my-mbti-results/how-frequent-is-my-type.htm.

encompassing, personality misunderstood by the vast majority.

Signs of an INFJ

Odds are if you have selected this book you probably have a pretty good idea that your partner is an INFJ. While there is no truly accurate manner of determining the Myers-Briggs personality type of another person, since it is a personal assessment which requires a great deal of self-reflection, there may be some signs that can help point to whether or not you are in a relationship with an INFJ.

Obviously the first indication would be that they have taken the test and have told you their type. In this case, going off of their personal assessment is a fairly safe guess. Though some do not always test accurately, there is no one better to assess a person than the person themself.

Some, however, are not certain of their type having never taken the assessment or they feel the results were inadequate. In these cases, you can look for some

> ## *Real Relationships*
>
> "INFJs have high, yet simple expectations when it comes to life and love with extremely complicated worlds that form around those expectations, dreams and hopes."
>
> ~ Anonymous INFP

general personality traits which may help you decide whether or not the person you are in or hoping to begin a relationship with is an INFJ. As always, it is important to remember that every individual is unique and no description of traits will ever fit entirely but offering guidelines and assessing generalities may assist in determining if you are on the right track.

Consider some of the following signs that your partner may be an INFJ. While each sign is not specific only to the INFJ personality, a combination of these traits is a strong indication that your partner may be an INFJ.

They constantly seek to improve your relationship. Whether through reading blogs and self-help books or searching out groups and seminars, the INFJ strives to reach an impossible standard for their relationships. This is not an indication that they are unhappy with the relationship, but rather that they cherish it so much that they wish to put enormous amounts of effort into making it the best it can be.

They respond to your emotions. INFJs are great listeners, but no matter what you say to them, they are more apt to respond to your emotions than to your words. If you are going on about a problem in your life, your INFJ partner may not seem interested at first in offering a solution but will jump right into helping you process how you feel about the situation. What starts as a brainstorming event to you may quickly turn into what seems like a therapy session as the INFJ exercises their Fe function and sets out to help you feel better.

They talk about the distant future. Try not to get too scared off if your partner jumps right to the long term scenarios of life. If they are an INFJ, simple discussions about whether or not to buy a shirt may turn into pondering about five years from now at cousin Suzie's wedding. INFJs are future-oriented thinkers whose brains are constantly scanning through various outcomes, which will be discussed in more detail in upcoming chapters.

Anything about the past may not be pertinent to the INFJ because the future is chock full of possibilities. Don't worry about them getting too vocal about picking out curtains in a couple of years because also floating around in their heads are the possibilities of what to do if you die in a fiery train wreck or how to pick up someone new in case it doesn't work out. This does not mean they are not serious about the relationship. Rather their brains are highly capable of carrying on many scenarios at once.

The negativity of the world overwhelms them. If sharing the negativity of the local news over the dinner table has your significant other seeming distant for the rest of the evening, they may be an INFJ. Just hearing news of a lost kitten can be hard for them and they need a little processing time. If you happen to mention something more intense, like a school shooting, expect to give them a little more space for dealing with their emotions.

They shut down. Sometimes for no apparent reason at all, if your partner seems to close themselves off to you indefinitely, it is possible they are an INFJ. Try not to take it personally and definitely do not push too hard to get them to open up as the harder you push, the further away they will drift. Sometimes general life can become too overwhelming for an INFJ, whether it is the negativity mentioned above, the millions of scenarios they run through their mind or just the everyday menial tasks of life, and they need to mentally escape from it all.

If these traits sound like your partner, then this book is sure to give you better insight as to how to interact with, understand and build an intimate relationship with the one who captures your heart.

INFJ Strengths

Every person brings with them to a relationship strengths and weaknesses. INFJs are no different. In order to foster a healthy balance within a relationship, it is important to recognize and embrace each positive and negative quality with unconditional love and compassion. In doing this, we are better able to use our own strengths to build up another's weaknesses.

Known to be natural humanitarians, the INFJ's strengths when recognized and appreciated by their partner, can help both members of the relationship flourish, bringing about a mutual firm base on which to build in the future.

As you read through the strengths mentioned here, consider your partner. Think about specific instances when they have exhibited these strengths in your relationship. Take a few moments to recognize how each strength encourages growth in your relationship.

Seeks Lifelong Relationships

INFJs crave deep and meaningful relationships. As individuals who wish to know the core of another human being rather than flitter around in shallow conversation, they want to reach the heart of those they meet.

It is because of this that they are not seeking one night stands or brief, superficial interactions. To do so would feel empty and pointless, offering no benefits or satisfaction to the INFJ. If your plans as you move forward are merely to seek a physical relationship, I recommend you seek elsewhere as the INFJ is not very likely to be interested in such an association. Rather, INFJs seek connection. Many are believers in soul mates and will not settle for anything less.

On top of their longing for deeper connections, INFJs tend to believe that there is good in everyone, seeing past imperfections or annoyances. As individuals who enjoy helping others improve themselves, the INFJ is more likely to help their significant other flush out areas of weakness or talk through relationship challenges. Patient and sympathetic, they will choose to work with their partner on improving themselves and their relationship when other types might just prefer to call it quits.

This ability to stick to relationships can easily shift from a strength of the INFJ to a weakness if they become heavily focused on fixing their partner or beginning a codependent cycle. But when both partners are looking to help one another be the best they can be for the long term, this INFJ trait is one to be cherished and admired.

Loyal and Trustworthy

INFJs are known for their strong moral character. They have deep-seated values which they are hold firmly, especially when it comes to those closest to them.

Because their relationships matter a great deal, loyalty and trustworthiness are at the top of their moral list.

Due to their depth of loyalty, INFJs have been called the Protector. Their passionate love for those closest to them calls them to stand up for and defend their loved ones at all costs.

Gossip, rumors and lies are not areas in which the INFJ chooses to spend their time. They would rather focus on building up those around them as opposed to tearing them down. As people with such a high level of loyalty, they are often confused by those who are dishonest or deceitful. They believe that everyone deserves the truth and any deceit is a grave injustice.

Since their standards of loyalty and trust are so high, the INFJ will hold their loved one to the same principles. Any instance of distrust or deceit and the INFJ will begin to close themselves off. But even in distancing themselves from the one who betrayed them, they will never abandon their own morals to respond in kind.

Warm, Compassionate and Selfless

Having a highly developed extroverted Feeling function makes it difficult for an INFJ to be anything other than kind and compassionate to those around them. This function allows them to closely tune in to the emotional state of others and adjust their behaviors accordingly. It is not uncommon for the INFJ to bend over backwards to ensure the complete comfort of their significant other as long as it does not require them to go against their own moral code.

INFJs exhibit a heightened level of empathy towards those around them which is amplified with those closest to them. They have a phenomenal ability to put themselves in the shoes of another, seeing things from their vantage point, which causes them to be compassionate to all living things.

As a person who feels at their best when they are helping others, the INFJ wants nothing less than to ensure that those around them feel good about themselves, content in their space and comfortable with life. Seeing others content is what makes an INFJ happy.

ire to Improve the Relationship

INFJs are perfectionists. They love to improve themselves and those around them and rarely feel satisfied with anything less than they have sought out to achieve. In their minds, everything has room for improvement. From reading books and magazines, attending seminars, retreats and workshops, or speaking with professional relationship counselors, the INFJ constantly seeks new information to help improve the relationship they hold so dear.

It is important to note, however, that this is not an indication that they are unhappy with your relationship, but rather that they cherish it so much they wish to put enormous amounts of effort into making it the best it can be.

This trait may manifest itself in a variety of different ways. The INFJ may spend a great deal of time working on self-care and personal improvements or growth. If they are a better version of themselves, they can be a healthier participant in the relationship. They might also offer assistance in helping you with areas of struggle. Their goal here is not to change or fix you, but to encourage you to be the best version of yourself you can be. They might also want to work together, trying new things and discussing new concepts in an attempt to bring your relationship to the next level. INFJs are not subscribers of the "if it ain't broke, don't fix it" mentality. They are more likely to say "if it ain't perfect, then keep fine-tuning it."

Excellent Conflict Resolvers

Though INFJs strongly dislike conflict of any kind, their natural ability to see many different sides of a situation paired with their remarkable people skills make them excellent conflict resolvers. As much as they love to see things working in harmony, they also value truth and transparency. Because of this, they tend to not be the type to sweep problems under a rug. They would rather work together to get to the heart of the matter and fix what is wrong to ensure that the situation does not continue to cause problems or fester beneath the surface.

Since they thrive at listening and empathy, they never shy away from a conversation about your feelings on a situation. Even if they disagree with your stance,

27

they are very likely to embrace the emotions you feel and help work together to find a comfortable solution.

Their Ni function makes them able to see a situation from many different angles which offers them a unique perspective on the problem before them. You may find yourself amazed by the solutions an INFJ is able to come up with, even in the heat of the moment.

Adaptable and Willing to Compromise

Similar to their compassionate and selfless nature, the INFJ is also very willing to compromise in a relationship. If the INFJ makes a decision that leaves someone they love uncomfortable or displeased, they are no longer able to enjoy their decision. Instead, they would rather make a choice that makes everyone feel content. Their Ni function makes them adept at recognizing the optimum solutions in most scenarios. When paired with their Fe, they are able to apply their solutions on a human level, making any necessary alterations to ensure both parties are comfortable and content with the outcome.

That being said, the INFJ is not one to be a doormat. Because they hold their core values so deeply, they are usually not willing to adapt to situations that would ask them to compromise or bend those values. If they are in a relationship with someone who frequently pushes these boundaries, red flags are sent up and the INFJ is likely to end the relationship.

Great Listeners

As previously mentioned, the INFJ thrives when helping those around them. If you find yourself needing assistance in any area, whether you just want to vent or are seeking advice and encouragement, then the INFJ in your life will always make themselves available. Apart from simply hearing your words, the INFJ is able to tune into underlying meanings or deeper awareness of your situation. They can feel unexpressed emotions and pick up on small inflections which others may require you to spell out. INFJs do not only listen, they hear, comprehend and engage in your words.

No matter how early you are in the relationship, opening yourself up and allowing them to be there for

29

you emotionally is sure to strengthen the bond and build trust. The only instance in which this would not be the case is if there is existing animosity between you and your INFJ partner. When they feel hurt or slighted, you are more likely to get the cold shoulder or silent treatment than a listening ear and reassuring shoulder. Be sure that you fish out and discuss any issues prior to coming to them for help or they may feel used as opposed to appreciated.

Supportive and Encouraging

INFJs love seeing others be the best versions of themselves in all aspects of life. Because of this, they are sure to support you in any venture that gets you excited and passionate, no matter what the stakes. As individuals who are able to see multiple outcomes, they can certainly envision your success on any undertaking and are likely to be right by your side cheering you on, provided your interests are genuine and moral.

Never be afraid to share your wants and desires as well as any plans to make them a reality. The INFJ loves to help you sort through plans and ideas and assist you in improving your life in any way you desire. INFJs are passionate cheerleaders and there is no one they would rather cheer on than those they care about the most.

As you can see, the INFJ in your life has many positive qualities that, when recognized and appreciated, can truly shine in any loving relationship. This list is far from exhaustive, so take a few moments before reading on to ponder other positive traits your partner exhibits and consider how those traits may relate back to their personality. You may find it a fun exercise in intimacy to discuss these traits with your partner as well as how their cognitive functions play a role.

$\mathcal{INFJ}$ $\mathcal{W}eaknesses$

INFJs are human beings, and just like all human beings, they carry with them weaknesses and negative traits which others may find less than favorable. Of course each individual's past will shape who they are and where they struggle but as a whole, INFJs do have areas which may be more challenging for them.

As I mentioned, the areas in which someone is more likely to struggle are often related to the lesser developed cognitive functions. The more under-developed a function, the more likely it is to lead to weaknesses, especially if it is not recognized and accepted. One's cognitive functions can give you some strong insight into the areas which need the most attention, much like exercising a muscle.

The INFJ in your life may cause you to see fireworks, hear the gentle tunes of a harpsichord and transport you to a meadow of lilies on a pristine spring day, making it difficult to ever believe that they have flaws. Or perhaps you are in a more challenging place in your relationship and you are wondering if the INFJ has anything but flaws. Both extremes are going to make the waters of your relationship a little choppier requiring greater effort to traverse. Instead, it is best to recognize that the INFJ is a human being with their share of positive and negative characteristics. Accepting their imperfections as well as taking the time to look at your own helps increase the chances of positive exchanges through understanding and acceptance rather than through deceptive rose-colored glasses or walls of disdain and bitterness.

While none of the struggles we are about to touch on are only ascribed to INFJs, you may even find that some of them do not apply to the one you fancy. Keep in mind as you are reading that each of these traits are discussed in order to give you a better understanding of why the INFJ may respond or function in the way they do, offering insight to help encourage mutual communication.

Mentally Elsewhere

You may notice that the INFJ in your life enjoys existing within their mind. They may appear quiet or distant on several occasions, not wishing to talk about what is rolling around in their heads. Perhaps they appear spacey, almost oblivious to the world around them.

While INFJs are introverts, leading to their love of retreating inside their heads, they seem to go a bit deeper into themselves than others are familiar with. Sometimes the INFJ's ability to shut off the world around them causes them to overlook obvious sensory details (like the wall they are about to walk into or the person beside them calling their name). Many INFJs consider themselves anything but graceful on a regular basis and can appear at times to have no experience operating the body in which they reside.

Real Relationships

"I am an ESTP female who is madly in love with an INFJ male. I love him to bits but it's a lot of hard work. We are different and I love our differences because he makes up for what I lack. However at times it gets too much. He'll be silent and have a concerned face and when I ask what's wrong, he would say 'nothing' but deep down I know that something is bothering him. I think I battle with drawing him out which I have realized that is something I have to be patient with."

~ Anonymous ESTP

This occurs most often when they are stressed, overwhelmed or tired and in need of a mental break. Because their least developed primary function is extroverted Sensing, it takes them a great deal of mental power to use this function consciously. When in need of a recharge, they shut off the more difficult pieces of their mind and rest comfortably in the most developed, introverted iNtuition.

Since the INFJ's eighth function is introverted Sensing, some report finding it difficult and sometimes impossible to read their own bodies, giving them the continuous appearance of not understanding how their body should operate, causing clumsiness and gracelessness.

As a weakness, this lack of sensory functions becomes most apparent in basic day-to-day tasks. They may struggle with paying the bills regularly, consistent upkeep of household chores, or remembering scheduled plans. INFJs can also lack a sense of direction. Sensory dominant individuals might find their inability to remember how to get from point A to point B a humorous display while others can see it as a frustrating personality flaw. Any task that requires them to step out of their heads no matter how fatigued they may be is a great struggle destined to lead them to failure.

After enough failures to keep up with the external world, an INFJ can be viewed as lazy or incompetent. If you expect them to juggle a large deal of sensory tasks on a regular basis without allowing for some time to escape deep inside their heads, they will begin to make simple mistakes and ultimately shut down.

The best combatant for this is first to offer acceptance of how their brains function. The natural intuitive talents and strengths of an INFJ are not readily accepted in comparison to sensing strengths, but changing your mindset to understand that they are using their strengths when just sitting and staring is a great way to also accept their weaknesses.

In many instances, INFJs are aware of this area of struggle even if they do not understand cognitive functions or what is occurring. They can be hard themselves, feeling frustrated for not being capable of staying present in the sensory world and completing regular tasks effortlessly. Offering acceptance can help them extend the same level of compassion to themselves, allowing them to better recover from fatigue and handle tasks when they need to be completed.

Of course, INFJs still need to complete basic responsibilities and not doing so is unhealthy within a relationship, both for their partner as well as themselves. When they are accepted for their need for down time, they feel comfortable in taking the mental escape necessary to recharge in order to have the energy required to work in their lesser developed functions.

Cold Exterior

INFJs are compassionate and warm individuals through and through. They are selfless and wish the best for all individuals around them with few conditions or contingencies. They long to invite everyone into their inner world, ready to offer a hypothetical warm cup of chamomile tea and encourage them to prop their feet up and share tales of years past. Their hearts exude genuine warmth and kindness.

Yet this soft, gentle interior is surrounded by a cold, stone exterior. This exterior exists in two layers: the invisible emotional layer which exists to protect their very vulnerable interior and the visible, bodily layer which appears stony simply because INFJs are at times unaware of their exterior.

The emotional layer is the piece that all INFJs carry which causes them to be slow to open up to those around them. Often misunderstood by others as well as themselves, INFJs reveal their warm interior in layers. Any sign of judgment or harshness from another causes them to shut down the remaining layers deep within themselves, never to be opened to that individual again.

39

When you experience this emotional layer of coldness, it may be off-putting causing you to wonder whether or not the INFJ has any interest in moving forward in a relationship. You may question their ability to be intimate and begin to wonder if they are the warm individual you thought them to be. If they continue to converse, offering slow pieces of themselves, chances are they are just taking their time to break down the layers. The INFJ is putting out feelers to see how their interior is received by you and each time you respond with kindness and acceptance, they will unravel another layer.

On the other hand, if the INFJ suddenly clams up during the conversation, not asking questions or offering information, this is a sign that they have shut you out. They may not be interested or you might have hurt them in some way. Getting them to open up their vulnerable interior could be an uphill challenge at this point.

The second cold layer is the visible layer. This layer is often misunderstood by those only first meeting the INFJ. As mentioned, INFJs enjoy retreating into their heads, unaware of their bodies or the world around them. With introverted Sensing as their eighth function, paying active attention to their physical self can not only be a struggle for the INFJ, but sometimes frustrate and anger them. Paying attention to normal social behaviors like smiling at every passerby or thinking about how to position your body in each scenario is a nuisance to INFJs and when they are not in the mood to put forth the effort through their Fe, they just don't. This exhibits itself as the cold physical exterior that can make their blank face appear angry, off-putting or bored.

The INFJ is a great living example of why you should not judge a book by its cover. In doing so, you may never have the opportunity to break past the cold-appearing walls and reach the amazing person within who really just longs to give everyone a mental hug.

Stubborn as a Mule

INFJs are used to being right. Their intuition helps them know things which others could never pick up on and many times, despite not being believed by others around them, circumstances will prove them correct. Because intuition works in ways we cannot understand, INFJs get to a point that they feel they just know things and have no reason or ability to explain why.

41

After a lifetime of knowing things and being proven right more often than not, the INFJ begins to trust their intuition above all else, making them less open to outside views and opinions. Once they have made up their mind based on their intuition, attempting to change it is like trying to get the earth to spin the other way.

On top of being hard-nosed in their intuition, INFJs also hold a very strong set of core values. These values are not necessarily based on logic or facts, a quality that may frustrate the more sensory-minded. The INFJ is likely to establish their values based off of their experiences meshed with their intuitive knowledge. Their core value system will almost always be based on the good of humanity as they are incapable of separating ideas from humankind.

Basing their values in personal intuition may make them appear skewed to those around them. Without any clear indication of how the INFJ establishes what their intuition says paired with the obvious inability of one person to know what is best for all of humanity, if an INFJ does not have a healthy grasp of their introverted Thinking function, their core value system may border on zealotry or obsession.

42

Shadow Self

In Jungian psychology, there is a piece of every individual which is referred to as the "shadow." Basically a shadow is the negative or dark side of one's personality which usually resides within the subconscious and creeps out unknowingly. Everyone has a shadow self and everyone's shadow is unique as it is often rooted in life experiences which have been repressed in order to protect the ego.

The shadow self is presented through the inferior (or fourth) function and comes out in times of stress, fatigue or general frustration. When stress or frustration occur, it causes one's inferior function to go into overdrive, dramatically affecting their personality, causing what is referred to as the "grip experience" (since it feels as though the inferior function takes ahold of them, making them unable to escape its grip).

Once in this grip, the INFJ may not appear anything like their normal self. In the book *Was That Really Me?: How Everyday Stress Brings Out Our Hidden*

Personality,[5] Naomi Quenk wonderfully illustrates how this shadow presents itself in the midst of the grip experience for an INFJ. She explains that the grip experience causes "obsessive focus on external data, overindulgence in sensual pleasure, and adversarial attitude toward world."

Usually these present themselves in a narcissistic manner, causing the INFJ to become combative and grandstanding even with those closest to them. They may shift to sensory obsession which can be exhibited through harmless modes such as watching sitcom reruns endlessly or playing mindless video games or they can be detrimental like overeating, substance abuse or sexual promiscuity.

While most slip in and out of their shadow function on a regular basis which is a healthy response to stress when channeled appropriately and for short periods of time, more extreme instances make it feel impossible for one to escape the grip of their inferior function. In these instances, it is best for the INFJ to take some time alone to recharge and reassess their

---

[5] Quenk, Naomi. *Was That Really Me?: How Everyday Stress Brings Out Our Hidden Personality*. Nicholas Brealey Publishing; 1st edition, 2002.

behavior. Giving them advice or seeking them out at this time would be disadvantageous to the relationship as it forces the INFJ deeper into the shadow self, potentially causing them to say and do things which may be irreparable.

After given a fair amount of time to regroup, the INFJ will most likely feel a great deal of shame and remorse for their behaviors. Back in the light of their dominant function, they will see all too clearly how they hurt or offended others or ways in which they harmed themselves.

Most INFJs will exhibit some pieces of the negative traits described in this section, but healthy individuals are able to recognize and take responsibility for them. If you are having some specific struggles with the INFJ in your life, consider these points and decide whether or not they are exhibiting these characteristics. Sometimes shedding light on the problem is enough to help work through it, both as an individual as well as a couple.

No one is perfect. Everyone has a balance of positive and negative characteristics which make up who they are. Determining whether or not these characteristics are something you are willing to live with or work through is a decision which only you can make.

INFJ Communication

Communication, whether you are just starting out or if you have been together for decades, is the *most* important aspect of a healthy, happy and fulfilling relationship. There is no shortage of literature designed to help couples improve their communication in order to cure the majority of relationship problems. How to speak to one another, unhealthy phrases or concepts, warning signs of negative talk and many other areas are discussed across the board to improve communication.

Learning about the communication style of another individual has a twofold effect: first, it allows you to better understand when they share their thoughts with you and second, you can tailor your words to be better received. Both methods allow for fewer miscommunications, helping you connect on a deeper level and feel safer discussing important topics.

When it comes to understanding the communication style of an INFJ, the first thing you need to recognize is that they are extremely slow to open up. Try not to take this piece personally nor let it deter you from moving forward in the relationship. In many instances, the INFJ is seeking someone who they feel comfortable exposing themselves to and are waiting for someone to come along who is a safe place to release their inner thoughts.

Once they feel comfortable, they will begin to unravel their layers. With each word they speak, they will be reading you for subtle cues, consciously and subconsciously. The slightest indication of judgment or disinterest will cause them to clam up almost immediately. This comes across as an abrupt end to a detailed exposé, perhaps by stating "never mind" or trailing off. Their demeanor will change and you may get the sense that they are angry or hurt.

Depending on exactly what caused the sudden cease in sharing, they either remain cold and closed off or may be open to discussing what happened. Consider why they may have closed themselves off. Do not be afraid to ask them. INFJs prefer direct discussions over game playing. If the offense was small, like a detection of disinterest, probing a little further will help them believe that you are genuinely curious about what they have to say. On the other hand, if it was something more extreme like blatant judgment or dismissal of their thoughts, getting them to open up again will prove challenging.

In either case, the best course of action is honesty and compassion. Any trace of fibbing, ill-intent or worse and the INFJ will close themselves off even more, perhaps never opening their heart again.

When conversation runs smooth and your interest and acceptance is clear, you may notice that your partner will go through periods of intense listening and quizzing you for personal information and periods of what sounds like rambling as they uncork the funnel of their thoughts. Communication is tremendously important to the INFJ. The INFJ desperately longs to be understood as well as to accurately understand. If they feel they may be misunderstood, they will either say nothing at all or they will spew an encyclopedia's worth of information to make sure they have covered all angles. The more they say, the more likely you matter a great deal to them. If you did not, they would opt instead for saying nothing.

Because being understood matters a great deal to the INFJ, they have a tendency to be overly precise with their words. They never wish to give half-truths or omissions that may leave room for misunderstandings or wrong ideas. Instead, the INFJ offers honest and genuine statements or responses, no matter how insignificant the discussion may be. For example, if asked whether or not they like seafood, the INFJ rarely opts for a straight yes or no. Instead, you may find yourself at the receiving end of a long line of answers in regards to individual types of seafood from caviar to shark. In the INFJ mind, simply answering "yes" since they enjoy most aquatic cuisines when they know, in fact, that they dislike calamari leaves them feeling dishonest.

> ## *Real Relationships*
>
> "I am an INFJ with experience in ENTJ/INFJ relations. When the ENTJ in my life says things to me that upset me, I have a tendency to walk away. He is also very interested in understanding me in order to not offend me in the same way. After I've given him some insight and reading material on INFJs, he's definitely a lot more aware of how I take things to heart. One thing that I admire about him is that he always makes an effort now to ask how I feel."
>
> ~ Anonymous INFJ

On top of their desire to give the truth, the whole truth and nothing but the truth, they also like to offer the roots of their thoughts. By this I mean that it is not enough for you to know whether or not they like seafood, they want you to know why. They may share a story about the first time they tried a dish, how they felt as they ate it, who they were with and so on.

Because your partner prefers accurate and complete responses to questions, being put on the spot for a quick response is anxiety-inducing. They strongly dislike being forced into immediate answers since it does not allow them to ponder all the angles and answer as thoroughly as they would like. In instances when this happens, it is not unlike them to offer the first answered that enters their mind only to contradict it or complete it later after they have been given the opportunity for deeper consideration. Allowing the INFJ time to answer questions, offering follow up questions at a later time and being accepting of any contradictory responses will put them at ease and make them feel comfortable opening up more in the future. On the other hand, calling them out on contradictions or questioning their honesty or integrity will cause them to worry about articulating precisely each time, making them stress over providing accurate responses and ultimately causing them to shut off their free flow of thinking. This cold-appearing response is a good sign that any future intimacy will be stifled.

An INFJ's line of thinking is rarely linear and their Ni function allows them to connect and interweave amazing levels of details which others may deem irrelevant but they feel are notable and important to the big picture. This makes it a challenge for the INFJ to be concise as they see importance even in the minor details. You may notice this as you tell a story, particularly if you tend to be direct and to the point. Your partner may begin to ask a series of little questions as they try to piece together a bigger picture.

INFJs also enjoy communicating in metaphors. With internal workings based mainly on feelings and intuition, putting things to words can be a struggle but they still yearn to express themselves. For this reason, they can paint an image with their words hoping to convey the correct feeling that they are experiencing within. Some may even find it easier to paint a literal picture, compose a song, or opt for poetic styles of communication if they are having a particularly difficult time finding simple words to express themselves.

On the flip side, the INFJ mind is very capable of being overly literal when listening to another communicate. They have a tendency to take the metaphors or emotions of another and interpret them into a literal understanding, much as scholars interpret Shakespearean works. I you are a metaphorical speaker, the INFJ will interpret your words and convey them literally to confirm that they understood you correctly. If you tend to be a literal straight shooter, the INFJ will ask several questions to pull out a deeper understanding of your point. While these two means of communication may seem contradictory, they are both rooted in the INFJ's longing to understand you on the deepest possible level.

Internal and External Processing

INFJs, like most introverts, prefer to process information internally before bringing it to the surface and sharing their thoughts. When a new thought or possibility comes into their mind, they may spend a great deal of time focusing on obtaining information, processing it through their intuition and getting to a comfortable place before wishing to discuss it.

However, as individuals whose auxiliary function is externally focused, it is not uncommon for them to hit a wall in their internal processing. Because of this, they seek out safe areas in which to exercise their Fe in order to fully comprehend a situation and make the best possible conclusion. While their Fe can be exercised through art, music or writing, having another individual to share ideas with is optimal.

Real Relationships

"I am an INFJ and I have married an ESTJ. We have a few key principles in sync (religion, kids, travel) but in our day to day lives we have almost nothing in common (half the time we don't even eat the same thing for supper) and it's wonderful. He's my best friend. My husband *needs* continuous social interaction, which gives me the time and space I need to be alone! Even before we knew our personality types we knew we were polar opposites. Family and friends have often asked us how we work so well being so different. My husband's answer is always, "We are like puzzle pieces. We have to be opposite to fit together." Of course it is a lot of work. I am *really* emotional – something he has no grasp on – and I often think he is cold towards people, but he stabilizes me and I make him more personable. He is one of the very few people I have ever been able to open up to… He is patient. He holds no judgment. He is forever confused by my emotional triggers: happy, sad, the whole lot (poor guy!). But he lets me carry on until I've exhausted them from my system. Sometimes it's crying, sometimes it seems like hysteria, sometimes I just zone out for ages. It took him a long time to realize and understand that this isn't me being emotionally unstable. I just need to offload the unwanted emotions I absorb from other people."

~ Anonymous INFJ

If they feel especially safe with you and willing to expose themselves, you might notice that their processing expressions are filled with contradictions, incomplete thoughts or non-sequiturs. When this happens, it is because they need to hear themselves say something before concluding whether or not they agree with it. They are essentially talking to themselves, using you as a sounding board. Once they are able to comfortably go through this external line of thinking, the INFJ can shift back inside their head and process more intuitive driven thinking until they come to a conclusion. For difficult situations, they may need to go through their internal and external processes a few times before feeling satisfied with their stance.

What does this mean for you? It may mean initial confusion as you listen to their emotions and uncertain thoughts, particularly if you find yourself a logical-minded individual. If you tend to be a predominantly extroverted Thinker, it would be common for you to assume that the INFJs expression are the whole of their logical thoughts, causing you to want to correct errors, point out contradictions and get them to a conclusion faster. Careful. This type of feedback to an INFJ's thoughts is more likely to frustrate them, making them feel as though you are not hearing them and slowing down their cognitive processing.

It also may be the case that the INFJ will catch you off guard with an extreme change. As their Ni feeds them new information constantly, their mind jumps into action processing it internally. They may go through this processing for quite some time prior to feeling comfortable expressing their thoughts. This means that, while your partner seems to be springing a radical change on you, it is actually something they have spent a great deal of time thinking about and it is not a new idea to them. Only when they are ready to process the emotions of a situation are they willing to discuss it.

Though it may feel like they are keeping intimate thoughts from you, this is not their intent. Try not to take their willingness to share thoughts on particular subjects personally. Odds are, they are still working on the internal processing and will be more than willing to share once they reach the external portion of their process.

Future Possibilities

INFJs live in a world of possibilities. They thrive on their ability to see life through many different angles. Unlike some personality types, there is no limit to what an INFJ can envision for the world around them. Regardless of what may have happened in the past or what direction signs may point to in the future, the INFJ can still come up with several diverse outcomes and directions for what is to come.

On top of their ability to see a multitude of opportunities, the INFJ is a future-oriented thinker. This means that they are constantly looking forward, looking at the next steps and what is to come. Often times, they have little use for information about the past and have been known to struggle with staying present in their current surroundings. Their minds dwell in the future and all the possibilities it may hold.

For this reason, the INFJ focuses on many outcomes of the relationship based on little to no current or past information. These outcomes can be anything from settling down in a home, picking out curtains and starting a family to struggling through a difficult argument ultimately ending the relationship to suffering a horrific accident that changes life as you know it.

Some of the scenarios thought up are actively focused on and others can just pop into the INFJ's mind in a seemingly uncontrolled manner. While one or two scenarios can appear likely, the rest may be more far-fetched and improbable. No matter where these thoughts of the future fall on the spectrum, to the INFJ, each one has at the very least, a miniscule, albeit highly unlikely, chance of actually occurring. To rule any out based on past experiences or basic logic seems dismissive and closed off for even the more logical-minded INFJ.

In moving forward with any relationship, the INFJ sees a level of intimacy in sharing these scenarios with you. Some they share freely and happily, as they are mutually beneficial and on track for your future together. If the relationship is moving forward comfortably with open discussions of the future, the INFJ enjoys conversing about the possibilities of settling down and making future plans. Talk of what is to come can be thrilling and exhilarating for the INFJ. You may notice that when the conversation is focused on forward

59

thinking, the INFJ's demeanor will shift to uplifting and excited as they discuss what is to come.

On the other hand, there are scenarios that they may keep more private or secretive. This could be either because they are embarrassed by the absurdity of some of their outlandish thoughts or because they are less than appealing and may not be received well. For example, if they have some radical idea about bumping into a major studio executive who instantly adores their abilities and wants to fly them across the globe to immediately start a high-paying , low responsibility position, complete with a free mansion, brand new car and security for life, they may feel a little embarrassed about bringing it up. They are aware of the odds that something like that will never happen, though they still enjoy fantasizing about the awesome possibilities of the future.

Other scenarios which they may keep secretive are less positive. These include futures that are outside of their control, like destructive car accidents, movie-style versions of natural disaster scenarios or even small scale situations like tripping on a curb and breaking a leg. Other scenarios include negative behavior on your part, like infidelity, becoming abusive or just flat out ending the relationship, regardless of how confident they may be in themselves and the current situation.

A future scenario thought up by the INFJ that may be difficult to understand is when they think up futures where they end the relationship even if they are completely content and have no desire to do so. While it seems illogical to ponder a future where they actively end a relationship in which they are currently happy, it is important to remember that INFJs do not always fantasize logically, nor are their fantasies always happy.

You may be wondering why the INFJ would want to spend their mental power focusing on unhappy future scenarios especially ones which seem impossible, illogical or unnecessary. Many times the INFJ is not sure of why they would focus on these situations either. One reason may be that they feel better when prepared. Thinking through every conceivable scenario allows them to decide how they would react or feel if placed in that position. Feeling prepared brings them a level of peace for what the future may bring, no matter how predictable or radical.

Another reason INFJs focus on a variety of outcomes is to help them understand how they genuinely feel about a current situation. While you may perceive envisioning the end of a relationship as a negative thing, it actually can strengthen their part of the relationship when considered. Feeling the emotions help to remind them how important the relationship is and focuses them on working hard to improve it. Picturing you dying a tragic death and feeling the depth of loss they would endure is their own way of telling themselves how much you mean to them. Future-oriented tragedies are the INFJ's unique way of helping themselves stay present and appreciate where they are now.

While the INFJ loves to consider the future and plan for all possible outcomes, they do not like feeling stifled or trapped by these fantasies. There is a fine line between their desire to talk about the possibilities and their fear that you may take these discussions as hard and fast plans to be executed immediately. If they share their desire to attend an event with you next year, that is not your cue to go out and buy the tickets immediately. When they discuss the idea of settling down forever on your third date, this is not a sign that you should run screaming in the other direction, nor should you run to the jeweler to buy the wedding bands.

On the flip side, if you also enjoy looking toward the future and discussing things to come, it is important that you classify these discussions as ideas or fantasies, not plans that you have set in stone. Keeping things open and free flowing while also offering genuine thoughts and opinions about the future to come are vital to keeping an INFJ talking about their fantasies and not worried to hear yours.

There are personalities who are more focused on the present or the past. If you are one of these types, discussing the future can be difficult and even frightening for you. Present thinkers tend to prefer living in the moment, not worrying about what is to come or fretting about things that have happened in the past. If you are a present thinker, you have little desire to plan for the future and thus your tendency may be to brush off the topic when the INFJ brings it up. This is painful for them. They see it as a dismissal of intimacy and a lack of interest in their thoughts.

As a present thinker, while you may not be interested in planning for the future, it is still important that you allow the INFJ to voice their thoughts on what may come. Take heart in knowing that they are not necessarily creating a plan, but simply wish to discuss the possibilities. By allowing them to talk about their various scenarios, you are helping them feel more prepared for the spontaneity you so long for in life. Giving them a safe space to share their thoughts on the future will strengthen their ability to stay with you in the present.

If you fancy yourself a past-oriented thinker then you tend to be the type who likes to look at patterns from what has occurred in the past in order to decipher what is most likely to occur in the present and future. In this case, you are probably not averse to discussing the future, but may not have patience for the fanciful outlandish ideas with which the INFJ can create. As they talk about scenarios that have a minimal chance of occurring or which do not fit the data you have accumulated from past experiences, you might want to inform them of the slim chances of these situations actually happening. This can feel dismissive to the INFJ, stifling their ideas of what the future could bring. In the case that they are excited about a potential future scenario, your logical assessment may leave them feeling hopeless and destroyed.

Past thinkers may have little interest in discussing futures that are not likely to happen. Your default is to correct the INFJ and steer the conversation back to reality. Instead, try just hearing them out. Letting them discuss all their possibilities helps them feel safe and emotionally prepares them to handle factual situations that will occur. Also, feel comfortable in sharing your own ideas based on past data. The INFJ will love to hear your future predictions based on data and facts as long as you remain open to their less likely scenarios as well.

Love Language

Understanding how to communicate with another on an intellectual level is a great start in pursuing a deeper connection, but it can only take you so far in the relationship. INFJs want meaningful conversations and love the connection verbal intimacy brings to a relationship, but it may not meet their emotional need to feel loved. This is where their love language comes into play.

Love language is a concept made famous by Dr. Gary Chapman in his book *The 5 Love Languages: The Secret to Love that Lasts.*[6] In this book, Dr. Chapman explains that each person has a preferred way to feel and express love for another individual. These languages are classified as words of affirmation, quality time, physical touch, acts of service and gift giving. If, for example, an individual prefers to show their love through words of affirmation, they may leave love notes, say "I love you" or offer compliments. Those with an acts of service love language may show their love through random acts of kindness or doing favors for another. By learning how your partner prefers to show and receive love, you can better meet their needs and ensure that you are communicating love in a way they can easily receive it and feel it.

There is no direct connection between one's MBTI and their love language. Any type could prefer any language, and some people are even fluent in two or three ways to show love. This is why it is important to

---

[6] Chapman, Gary. *The 5 Love Languages: The Secret to Love that Lasts.* Northfield Publishing; Reprint edition, 2015.

learn and communicate one another's love languages in order to meet this need on a personal level.

Physical Intimacy

INFJs have a strong desire to please the ones they love in every aspect of the relationship including physically. However, due to the INFJ's lesser developed extroverted Sensing function paired with their poor shadow introverted Sensing function, they have a tendency to feel very disconnected from the physical world around them. While they have a deep longing to connect with their partners in a spiritual sense, some INFJs may struggle with showing this physically.

This is not to say that INFJs dislike or disconnect from physical intimacy. It is possible for an INFJ to have a physical love language and show their love best through physical touch. But when an INFJ does interact physically, it is always with great emotional depth. They view sexual intimacy as a spiritual experience rather than becoming engulfed in the physical actions.

Sexual pleasures are only fulfilling to the INFJ when their mind is fully connected to the moment. In some instances, the physical embrace is not even needed in order for them to feel the depth of sensual connection of which they crave. It is not uncommon for an INFJ to have extensive fantasies about their lover. Often times, the moment when they are most aroused or craving sexual intimacy can be when their partner is nowhere around, since as introverts the solitude allows them to be most in-tune with their emotions. As they have very vivid thoughts and imaginations, they can feel even more connected to their loved one when they are submerged in their minds. If you notice that your INFJ partner is more intimate after a stint of solitude, this may be the reason.

With that said, INFJs live to please those they love so it if physical intimacy is important to their partner then they strive to meet that need. They view sexual pleasures as a way to express the emotions they can so easily bring to mind in a shared way with their partner. If, for some reason, the INFJ does not or cannot meet the physical needs of their partner, they will feel a great amount of guilt or failure, wishing they were better able to please.

Since physical intimacy is so deeply intertwined with thoughts and emotions, casual encounters are near impossible for an INFJ. Most of them find it to be a pointless use of energy. Engaging in an empty physical encounter, even if it is as small as a kiss, frustrates the INFJ just as much as shallow conversation. If, however, an INFJ does engage in a seemingly emotionless fling, one of the following two scenarios may be at play.

The INFJ may attach manifested emotions to the other person, believing that perhaps there is a deeper connection there than initially recognized. Since they will have no logical basis for these manifested emotions, they might begin to believe it is their intuition talking, in which case they put themselves in a dangerous position as perceived intuition can be a powerful force to the INFJ.

If you feel the INFJ becomes more emotionally intense after a sexual encounter or if they seem connected during a physical act but pull away at other times, it may be possible that there are some attached manifested emotions involved. It is important to

69

encourage them to take some time to reflect on their emotions. Intuition speaks the loudest when we are quiet, alone and still. If they are in the heat of a moment when they suddenly believe there is a connection, odds are slim that it is their intuition speaking. Consider holding off on physical relations as you move forward.

On the other hand, if an INFJ is aware of the emptiness of a sexual encounter, they are more likely to use the sex as a method of self-abuse or punishment for something they believe is "wrong" with them. This can stem from past abuse, low self-esteem or self-worth or a means of escaping a current reality in which they want temporary relief. In these cases, the INFJ will exhibit their shadow functions which come out in a very negative manner. These functions exhibit themselves in overindulging in physical experiences as a means to escape their mind and intuition. INFJs always need to be aware of indulgences in the physical world as this is a large sign that they are not emotionally balanced.

Asexual INFJs

It is not uncommon for INFJs to identify themselves as asexual beings. Asexual is a term often misrepresented as a person who is turned off by or offended by any sexual encounter, but the truth is that an asexual individual simply does not experience physical sexual attraction. As INFJs often find themselves disconnected from their body or the physical world around them, it comes as no surprise that they would relate to asexuality.

Asexual INFJs may find great connections among others who prefer profound discussions rather than intercourse as a means of fulfilling their intimate desires. There are many groups out there geared specifically for helping asexuals find meaningful, lifelong relationships.

In the case that you are a sexual being in a relationship with an asexual INFJ, do not lose hope. Great communication about one another's needs, wants and dislikes are of utmost importance. No one wants to feel unloved and INFJs certainly do not want to leave their partner unfulfilled. Unwanted contact is never acceptable, but through proper discussion, many are able

71

to make a compromise and have a successful sexual/ asexual relationship.

Sexual or physical experiences to an INFJ are something that they do with great purpose of showing love for another. If you are in a committed relationship with an INFJ, recognize that everything from a brief kiss to passionate love-making is perceived as an intensely spiritual experience of expressing feelings and should never be taken lightly.

Fostering Intimacy

While there are many pieces of a relationship that must come together to make it work, all of these components need to be laid upon the foundation of intimacy. Without intimacy, all lines of communication shut down and no form of love can truly be expressed. Intimacy is when both partners are completely open and vulnerable with one another. Whether it is emotionally, mentally or physically, none can ever fully give themselves to another without the raw transparency which only comes from an intimate place.

No matter what stage of the relationship you are currently in, intimacy must be built and sustained in order for any forward progress to be made. Every person has a unique way of showing and achieving intimacy within their relationships. No two relationships will be exactly the same. Just like every other aspect of a personality type, INFJs have many things in common when it comes to what they need in order to feel comfortable and confident in letting their guard down and allowing themselves to become vulnerable and intimate.

Honesty and Trust

A relationship without honesty and trust is guaranteed to fall flat fairly quickly. Some personality types look at honesty and think of the bigger things, like financial transparency or fidelity. With an INFJ, the need for trust and honesty runs much deeper.

Because of their highly tuned intuition, INFJs have an incredible ability to read people. Whether consciously or subconsciously, the INFJ is constantly reading the people around them, from those they just met to those they have known for years. This means that they are more likely to catch the tiny fibs you may throw out, no matter how well-intentioned.

INFJs are interested in people's motives and curious about why they do the things they do. When they catch you in a small lie, they cannot help but wonder why you would choose that route. Though they may never call you on the lies they have caught, the INFJ will ponder the good scenarios and the bad scenarios, all ending in the same conclusion: lack of trust. Any time an INFJ catches a lie, regardless of its size or importance, they mentally file it away. As this file grows, as too does their trust deplete, never to be regained.

In order to ever have a chance at intimacy with an INFJ, the first and most important thing is to be completely transparent, honest and genuine at all times. If you do not like her dress, don't say you do. If you hated his mother's lasagna, don't smile and ask for the recipe. Little things count.

The INFJ is not interested in the subtle niceties and societal game playing. They want to see who you are, no matter how good or bad. They would rather see your worst parts exposed than wonder why you are trying to hide them.

Trust is everything to an INFJ.

Empathetic and Accepting

INFJs are over-flowing with empathy. Their levels of understanding the emotional state of another far surpass what you may believe capable. While you may easily be able to sympathize with another, the INFJ feels *exactly* what others are feeling. It can be a terrifying and lonely thing to an INFJ to see someone in pain and ache along with them while others overlook the suffering.

Because of this, practicing empathy is essential. If you are cold to someone in suffering, the INFJ will feel as though you are being just as cold to them, pushing you away as opposed to bringing you closer. The INFJ is craving someone who can understand and accept their high levels of empathy without assuming something is wrong or that they are too sensitive or need to toughen up. They want someone who sees their empathy and believes it is a beautiful, compassionate thing. They feel so alone in how empathetic they are so having someone who believes them, even if you cannot understand, goes a long way in helping them feel a little less alone.

Take a moment to imagine something in your life that means everything to you. Something that defines a piece of your personality. Maybe it is a hobby, your career, a genre of music, a favorite sports team, your heritage. No matter what it may be, call it clearly to mind. Now picture having a conversation with your special someone and bringing up this defining piece of you. Imagine that they scoff at it, insult it, or insinuate that this piece of your personality was a project they could undertake and "fix." Worse, imagine that they tell you that they do not believe you. They don't believe you really have the job you say you do or that you are really the heritage you claim to be. Would you leave that conversation feeling closer to your loved one? Odds are it would put a bad taste in your mouth, probably leaving you slightly fearful of opening up any more.

This is what the INFJ experiences often. When they attempt to foster intimacy and transparency by explaining to others their level of empathy, they are met with the notion that they need to toughen up or be fixed. It is not uncommon for people to tell them that their experiences are not possible or that it is all in their head. It pushes them away further from those individuals, leading them to shut down and no longer wish to open up any further. The area that most defines them is the very area that no one will accept, causing them to feel very alone.

In order to foster a deep intimate relationship with an INFJ, it is imperative that you believe and accept their level of empathy. When they begin to share the piece of them that cringes at any injustice, weeps at any pain and turns away from any horror, accept it with open arms. Recall the most empathetic you have ever been and attempt to sympathize with them on any level possible. Never insinuate that something is wrong with them or that they are too sensitive. Rather, embrace that they *are* sensitive and that is one of their best qualities.

Genuine and honest acceptance of who they are will go a long, long way in developing any intimate relationship with an INFJ.

Security and Stability

Despite the fact that the INFJ is a judicial personality type who appears to have it all together on the outside, their mind can be a chaotic, confusing and overwhelming mess. Some days are better than others and they feel grounded and at ease, but in an instant, something can happen that throws them into mental turmoil, leaving them grasping for anything to plant themselves firmly back on the ground.

In order to keep them from spinning out of orbit, the INFJ craves routine. As much as their intuition may pull them in and out of structure, they need a plan to get through the day. Any sudden and unexpected changes leave them feeling ill-prepared and send them directly back into exhausting mental chaos while they attempt to consider all scenarios simultaneously.

If you are the type who loves chaos or enjoys throwing wrenches in the plans, you will quickly exhaust an INFJ. It will not take long for them to view you as unstable and unpredictable, leaving them hyperaware in your presence, constantly scanning scenarios to stay ahead of what you may spring on them next. After living this way long enough, their anxiety will increase and they will see you as the source of their discomfort.

Some personality types are simply not planners, particularly the types who live in the moment. They thrive on the unexpected and enjoy chaos. ESFPs and ESTPs are great examples as their dominant function is extroverted Sensing, leaving them craving stimuli and unhappy if left unfulfilled.

If you tend to be less of a planner and find yourself struggling with stability, take heart. It does not make the relationship impossible, just slightly more challenging. Becoming aware of the INFJ's need for stability can make a world of difference in helping to offer it, even if you are the furthest thing from stable. When an INFJ is not overwhelmed and overloaded, a little unexpected change can be a good thing, with some stipulations:

- **Time:** Sudden change is the worst kind of change to an INFJ, so if you want to be spontaneous, choose things that offer a little solitary preparation time for your partner. Allowing them ten minutes to gather their thoughts in a safe place can help them prepare for the new scenarios and adventures.

- **Choice:** Opt for things that do not require them to change their schedule if they do not want to. If the INFJ feels forced into change, they may begin to feel angry and bitter toward you for the decision. Giving them a choice will help them feel in control, allowing for more security.

- **Understanding:** Do not pressure them or punish them for choosing to opt out of the spontaneity. Knowing that they have the safety and security of saying "no" when they please will make them more likely to say "yes" another time and they will feel respected and loved no matter their choice.

The INFJ is not looking for a dull and menial existence and despite their love of plans, they do have the ability to enjoy the unexpected on occasion. But it is important that they view you as a secure and stable individual who is not going to spring things on them at every turn. By respecting the above stipulations, even the most spontaneous person can become predictable and expected, allowing the INFJ to let their guard down and feel more secure.

Positivity

INFJs easily pick up the moods of those around them and can be deeply affected by negative emotions. Of course, life is filled with ups and downs but if they are constantly around someone who exudes negativity on a regular basis, this will act as a toxin to their soul.

As fixers by nature, constant pessimistic attitudes may at first attract an INFJ. Their kneejerk response is to dote on those who are struggling, offering mounds of genuine compassion and assistance. It is not uncommon for them to remain in relationships with a struggling individual in hopes of them one day turning around. At the beginning of the courtship, the INFJ's compassionate nature and uplifting personality can outshine the negativity. But that same negativity, if not corrected, will slowly creep into them, sapping them of

Real Relationships

"My ENFP personality is all about being positive and fully optimistic. When I can be positive for the both of us and not let my wife's pessimism affect me, wonderful things happen and we find a solution to the problem. But when I am negative and insecure, it does not go well."

~ Anonymous ENFP

the very caring that began the relationship, draining them until there is nothing left.

In order to avoid this slow drain of self, the INFJ needs someone who offers positivity and uplifting encouragement. This is not to say you cannot have a bad day or even a bad year. The difference is that you actively try to improve yourself and receive the compassion of the INFJ with purpose as opposed to seeing it as a source to tap dry.

It is important to note that false positivity is no substitute for genuine emotion. INFJs do not absorb false emotions. Even if they may believe them on the surface, their subconscious as well as their intuition will be able to pick up on the negativity.

As individuals who can see bigger picture and a multitude of possibilities, INFJs may appear pessimistic at times. By offering positivity, it helps them bring their overwhelming emotions back into check and see the reality of a situation instead of dwell on the anxiety-inducing outcomes that their mind may conjure up.

In any relationship there are ups and downs and being with someone who can help you up when you are down or lean on you when they need a lift is a treasured gift. Stay genuine and communicate when you are struggling, but do not let the INFJ's compassion become negativity's crutch or else there will be no compassion left to give.

Self-Awareness and Competence

INFJs are exceedingly self-aware, almost to a fault. They frequently reflect on their thoughts, behaviors and emotions, wondering where they can improve and fine-tune themselves. While they may have a great deal of self-awareness, they are even more aware of others, easily seeing ways to help and encourage people to become their best selves. INFJs thrive on helping people fix their problems and feel good about their lives.

Sometimes, however, the INFJ can do this to a fault. They become wrapped up in the people around them who need assistance, no matter how toxic those individuals may be. INFJs never want to stop helping those who wish to be helped, leaving them drained when that person is perpetually unhealthy.

In order to have a healthy level of intimacy with an INFJ partner, you should not be a taker who relies on or continuously seeks out the INFJ to help you or fix your problems. It may work in the short term to keep them by your side, but ultimately the INFJ will feel burnt out, shut down and begin to distance themselves from you until there is barely an ounce of intimacy left.

An INFJ who is required to be excessively focused on their partner will have nothing left to offer in terms of intimacy because their own sense of self becomes absorbed by the other person's needs. No relationship is healthy when there is codependent behavior. Both partners must be capable of self-awareness and competence in order to work on and handle their own problems as well as seek to improve themselves for the sake of the relationship.

If you desire a strong level of intimacy and mutuality within the relationship, you must take some time for self-reflection prior to moving forward. Looking at yourself as objectively as possible and searching for personal faults and weaknesses that you may bring to the relationship can give you a launching point to better self-care. Consider signs of codependence, whether obvious or subtle, that may be causing the INFJ to hold back pieces of themselves. If self-awareness is not an area in which you feel capable or comfortable, seek outside help from a coach or therapist.

The goal here is not to become perfect or change your persona. The INFJ loves unconditionally. Rather, your focus should be on taking the responsibility of fixing your problems or weaknesses off of your partner and placing them back onto your shoulders. The more you take responsibility for yourself, the more relaxed the INFJ will feel, allowing them to offer a greater level of intimacy.

Patience

If you take away one thing from this book, let it be this: *INFJs need patience.* As we have established, they are not impulsive, they do not like to be vulnerable and they are extremely complex individuals. These three components cause them to open up very slowly.

It is not uncommon for those seeking a relationship with an INFJ to wonder if they will ever truly know them or crack their "shell." The truth is, you could be in a relationship with an INFJ for decades and still discover pieces of their personality they have yet to disclose. They are not secretive or mysterious for any elusive or deceptive purposes. In fact, quite the opposite is true. INFJs are honest and transparent once they feel comfortable or safe with an individual. It is because of this transparency that simple exchanges leave them feeling vulnerable. They are not interested in half-told answers, but would rather be as comprehensive as possible in every response.

If asked about their childhood, the INFJ could prefer to clam up as opposed to give minor details.

87

While some early in a relationship would offer simple responses like where they grew up or what their father did for a living, the INFJ longs to tell all. Because this would leave them vulnerable to someone not yet deemed trustworthy, they opt to say nothing instead.

Real Relationships

"Be patient and do not criticize them by any means. Ask, suggest, surprise, be honest, dedicated and share that deep inner world within you and you will be amazed how beautiful life can be."

~ N.C. (INFP)

INFJs are emotional beings, making them feel sentimental in expressions. Because their words can be laced with raw emotion, answering logical questions feels exposed, divulging deeper meaning than they may be ready to offer.

Another aspect of being so complex is that many INFJs still have not yet figured themselves out. Constantly pondering, learning, self-reflecting and seeking greater meaning and understanding, INFJs are always reaching into their layers and discovering more and more of who they are. Patience is required in order to allow them to wade through the depth of their minds before they can offer a glimpse to you.

INFJs fancy themselves open books, wishing to expose their souls and reach past the shallowness of our current society. But with that comes a self-protection and a need to feel comfortable and safe before they allow themselves to be so vulnerable. If you are able to offer them the time and patience they need to fully come to trust you, you will have gained the most important key to unlocking the chambers of their soul, one piece at a time.

Working as a Pair

Everyone seeking a meaningful relationship wishes there was a magic formula which could easily tell them their perfect match. We dream of a system that could direct you away from the wrong person and into the arms of the right one, ensuring that they were the one for you.

Many psychologists have attempted to crack the love code but always seem to fall short. In every case there is an exception to the rule, usually several, which prove that there is no one way to decide if two individuals were meant to be.

In Myers-Briggs psychology, the quest to discover the perfect matches continues. Each has their own theory – from David Keirsey's opposites attract theories to Dr. John Beebe's "inverse relationships" – which may appear to hold some validity from a scientific standpoint but, just as it always has been, love remains a complex, mystifying terrain that leaves every theorist standing there scratching their head.

Depending on what book or article you read, you will find different versions of what the best and worst matches are for a successful relationship. Dr. John Beebe

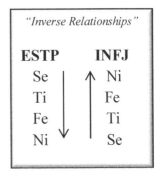

"Inverse Relationships"

ESTP	INFJ
Se	Ni
Ti	Fe
Fe	Ti
Ni	Se

applies a theory of "inverse relationships"[7] which is based on his studies of Carl Jung's inferior function archetypes – the "anima" holds a man's inferior function and the "animus" holds a woman's. This theory essentially states that partners with inverted primary functions are the best match as they offer a great deal of patience and tenderness towards those who use their inferior function. In this case, the ESTP would be the

---

[7] Beebe, John Ph.D. *Integrity in Depth (Carolyn and Ernest Fay Series in Analytical Psychology)*. Texas A&M University Press; New edition. 2005.

ideal match for an INFJ offering patience to the INFJ's Se function and vice versa.

On the other hand, David Keirsey in his book *Portraits of a Temperament*[8] creates a formula which is explained less through functions and more through the original Myers-Briggs dichotomies. Keirsey hypothesized that the ideal pair can be found by matching the second letter of one's personality type to another's while applying the opposite to the third and fourth letters. This means that an INFJ's ideal pairing would be either an ENTP or an INTP as shown in the box below.

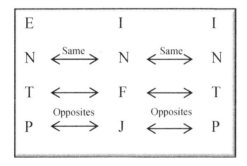

For centuries man has been searching for the perfect balance between the notion that opposites attract and commonalities comingle. Ultimately each person, regardless of their personality type, is so incredibly

---

[8] Keirsey, David. *Portraits of a Temperament*. Prometheus Nemesis Book Company; 3rd edition. 2004.

unique that no formula can offer a simple solution. The only true way to discover whether or not you are compatible with someone is through communication and dedication. There is no best or worst personality pairing; simply two individuals who need to make the conscious decision to put the necessary amount of effort into their relationship.

Comparing Your Functions

Having a better understanding of how the INFJ's heart and mind work can help you to move forward in your relationship with your INFJ partner. But this information will only take you so far unless you are better able to understand your own personality type and cognitive functions. It is highly recommended that you take the MBTI assessment as well as research your own personality type in order to discover how your mind receives, processes and communicates information with others.

While each MBTI personality type would need a book of their own to fully discuss their functional stack, here I wish to offer a quick glimpse at each type's functions to give you a launching point to better understand how you may see the world differently from your INFJ partner.

In the charts on the next few pages, find your personality type and note your primary and shadow processes in comparison to your INFJ counterpart's. You can go to page 104 in the appendix for a brief explanation of what each process means. As you look through your chart, note the differences and similarities between your functions. Do you share a primary function or is it the opposite? Do your functions appear in the INFJ's shadow or primary processes? Do the INFJ processes force you to use less developed functions or do they complement one another (i.e. Ne complementing Ni or Fe complementing Fi)?

Take the time to consider past discussions with your partner. Apply your new knowledge of functions to the conversation, using it as a lens to break down where there may have been miscommunications or strong understandings. Consider how you effortlessly use your dominant function. Where does it fit in with your strengths? How does your auxiliary function complement your dominant process? Is your tertiary process well-developed or can you see it as a personal weakness, in need of some nurturing?

Once you become aware of your cognitive functions, it will take time to easily recognize how they play out in your daily life. By staying cognizant of both your functions as well as your INFJ partner's, you gain the ability to look at discussions in a new light.

Next time you see a disagreement coming or struggle with understanding your partner's point of view, look back at these pages and attempt to see one another's perspective. As you forge ahead in the discussion, staying aware of your differences and weaknesses will help offer a level of patience and understanding in the conversation.

Remember that there is no one personality type that best matches an INFJ's functions. Every personality pairing is able to make their relationship successful if both are committed to understanding one another and working together to focus on strengths and improve weaknesses.

ESTP & INFJ	
Primary	*Primary*
Se	Ni
Ti	Fe
Fe	Ti
Ni	Se
Shadow	*Shadow*
Si	Ne
Te	Fi
Fi	Te
Ne	Si

ESFP & INFJ	
Primary	*Primary*
Se	Ni
Fi	Fe
Te	Ti
Ni	Se
Shadow	*Shadow*
Si	Ne
Fe	Fi
Ti	Te
Ne	Si

ISTJ & INFJ	
Primary	*Primary*
Si	Ni
Te	Fe
Fi	Ti
Ne	Se
Shadow	*Shadow*
Se	Ne
Ti	Fi
Fe	Te
Ni	Si

ISFJ & INFJ	
Primary	*Primary*
Si	Ni
Fe	Fe
Ti	Ti
Ne	Se
Shadow	*Shadow*
Se	Ne
Fi	Fi
Te	Te
Ni	Si

ENTP & INFJ	
Primary	*Primary*
Ne	Ni
Ti	Fe
Fe	Ti
Si	Se
Shadow	*Shadow*
Ni	Ne
Te	Fi
Fi	Te
Se	Si

ENFP & INFJ	
Primary	*Primary*
Ne	Ni
Fi	Fe
Te	Ti
Si	Se
Shadow	*Shadow*
Ni	Ne
Fe	Fi
Ti	Te
Se	Si

INTJ & INFJ	
Primary	*Primary*
Ni	Ni
Te	Fe
Fi	Ti
Se	Se
Shadow	*Shadow*
Ne	Ne
Ti	Fi
Fe	Te
Si	Si

INFJ & INFJ	
Primary	*Primary*
Ni	Ni
Fe	Fe
Ti	Ti
Se	Se
Shadow	*Shadow*
Ne	Ne
Fi	Fi
Te	Te
Si	Si

ESTJ & INFJ

Primary	Primary
Te	Ni
Si	Fe
Ne	Ti
Fi	Se
Shadow	*Shadow*
Ti	Ne
Se	Fi
Ni	Te
Fe	Si

ENTJ & INFJ

Primary	Primary
Te	Ni
Ni	Fe
Se	Ti
Fi	Se
Shadow	*Shadow*
Ti	Ne
Ne	Fi
Si	Te
Fe	Si

ISTP & INFJ

Primary	Primary
Ti	Ni
Se	Fe
Ni	Ti
Fe	Se
Shadow	*Shadow*
Te	Ne
Si	Fi
Ne	Te
Fi	Si

INTP & INFJ

Primary	Primary
Ti	Ni
Ne	Fe
Si	Ti
Fe	Se
Shadow	*Shadow*
Te	Ne
Ni	Fi
Se	Te
Fi	Si

ESFJ & INFJ

Primary	Primary
Fe	Ni
Si	Fe
Ne	Ti
Ti	Se

Shadow	Shadow
Fi	Ne
Se	Fi
Ni	Te
Te	Si

ENFJ & INFJ

Primary	Primary
Fe	Ni
Ni	Fe
Se	Ti
Ti	Se

Shadow	Shadow
Fi	Ne
Ne	Fi
Si	Te
Te	Si

ISFP & INFJ

Primary	Primary
Fi	Ni
Se	Fe
Ni	Ti
Te	Se

Shadow	Shadow
Fe	Ne
Si	Fi
Ne	Te
Ti	Si

INFP & INFJ

Primary	Primary
Fi	Ni
Ne	Fe
Si	Ti
Te	Se

Shadow	Shadow
Fe	Ne
Ni	Fi
Se	Te
Ti	Si

Conclusion

Imagine a world where we could read our partner's mind. One where they could understand our needs and desires immediately. No miscommunications or mis-understandings. Petty arguments would become pleasant conversations. Both partners would feel equally loved at all times.

It is a world which every couple longs for, particularly on the rough days. Each person wishes they could be understood without uttering a word and loved without question.

As of now, there is no technology or magic potion that makes this a reality. Unless or until that day arrives, the only way to come close to such a harmonious relationship is through seeking a better understanding of our partner's perspectives.

Myers and Briggs have offered us a window into the minds of others. The more we study the cognitive processes of a personality type, the more effective our communication can be, allowing us to pull back the drapes of the window and glimpse into the unique mind of our partner.

At every stage of a relationship, there is no better substitute to achieve healthy intimacy than listening and truly understanding. It is my hope that this book has offered you a better understanding about the mind and perspective of an INFJ in order to help you learn to communicate with your partner and reach a greater level of intimacy.

What's Next?

Gaining this deeper understanding is only the first step to strengthening your relationship. If you have not all ready, I recommend learning about your own personality type and cognitive processes and how they play a large role in your strengths, weaknesses and communication style.

From there, take this knowledge and start a conversation with your INFJ partner. Help them understand your processes and listen as they share about theirs. Working as a team, with patience, understanding and empathy, help one another strengthen your weak functions and enhance your strong ones. By arming yourselves with knowledge and listening and truly communicating, you can work as a team to become healthier, well-rounded individuals, better understanding each other's minds and forever unlocking your hearts.

Common Acronyms

MBTI – Myers-Briggs Type Indicator

I – Introvert/Introverted

E – Extrovert/Extroverted

N – iNtuitive/iNtuiting

S – Sensor/Sensing

T – Thinker/Thinking

F – Feeler/Feeling

J – Judicial/Judging

P – Perceiver/Perceiving

Ni (introverted iNtuition) – ability to think abstractly, globally, thoroughly and complexly, noticing patterns and information others are unable to see.

Fe (extroverted Feeling) – connecting with others, acting in ways that make others feel comfortable and pleased, mainly through warmth, graces and good manners.

Ti (introverted Thinking) – analyzing, internal reasoning and categorizing, noticing and remembering small details, behaviors and evidence.

Se (extroverted Sensing) – awareness of external sensory details, desire to accumulate data sensory input.

Ne (extroverted iNtuition) – interpreting hidden meanings, brainstorming ideas and interweaving small details to form a larger picture.

Fi (introverted Feeling) – weighing information against a core belief system and assigning value and significance to all things.

Te (extroverted Thinking) – organizing, sequencing and planning ideas and environments based on logic and facts.

Si (introverted Sensing) – Storing and retrieving detailed facts and weighing them against current situations.

Additional Reading

Jung, Carl. *Psychological Types*. Princeton University Press, 1976.

Briggs Myers, Isabel & Mary H. McCaulley. *Manual: A Guide to the Development and Use of the Myers-Briggs Type Indicator*. Consulting Psychologists Press, 1985.

Quenk, Naomi. *Was That Really Me?: How Everyday Stress Brings Out Our Hidden Personality*. Nicholas Brealey Publishing; 1st edition, 2002.

Chapman, Gary. *The 5 Love Languages: The Secret to Love that Lasts*. Northfield Publishing; Reprint edition, 2015.

Keirsey, David. *Portraits of a Temperament*. Prometheus Nemesis Book Company; 3rd edition. 2004.

ALSO LOOK FOR

The Empathic INFJ:
Awareness and Understanding for the
Intuitive Clairsentient

This book, when paired with *The Empathic INFJ Workbook: Tools and Strategies for the Intuitive Clairsentient*, will offer you a functional and focused guide to understanding your level of empathic abilities and help you learn and establish new tools and techniques to thrive in your day to day living.

Complete with descriptions, resources and tools, grab you copy today!

A Look Inside a Rare Mind:
An INFJ's Journal through Personal Discovery

A raw look into the mind of an INFJ through the beginning stages of her journey from first discovering her Myers-Briggs Personality Type.

This book is a descriptive personal journal shared to help those who are at the beginning stages of discovering that they, too, are an INFJ and may be searching for validation, understanding and a kindred spirit.

For more information about these works as well as future publications, please visit jennifersoldner.com.

Made in the USA
Middletown, DE
26 May 2019